T0011666

FIGHT FOR LIFE!

Rain Forest Survivor

BY **James Buckley Jr.**

ILLUSTRATED BY **Cassie Anderson**

BEARPORT
PUBLISHING

Minneapolis, Minnesota

BEAR CLAW

Credits

Cover art by Cassie Anderson

Photos: 20T © Pisut Chounyoo/Shutterstock; 20B © Blue Planet Studio/Shutterstock; 21B © Spayder Pauk 79; 21T © New Africa/Shutterstock; 22T © Liudmyla Boleva/Dreamstime.com; 22B © A41Cats/Dreamstime.com; 23 © Eric Isselee/Shutterstock.

Bearport Publishing Company Product Development Team

President: Jen Jenson; Director of Product Development: Spencer Brinker; Senior Editor: Allison Juda; Editor: Charly Haley; Associate Editor: Naomi Reich; Senior Designer: Colin O'Dea; Associate Designer: Elena Klinkner; Product Development Assistant: Anita Stasson

Produced by Shoreline Publishing Group LLC
Santa Barbara, California
Designer: Patty Kelley
Editorial Director: James Buckley Jr.

DISCLAIMER: This graphic story is a dramatization based on true events. It is intended to give the reader a sense of the narrative rather than a presentation of actual details as they occurred.

Library of Congress Cataloging-in-Publication Data

Names: Buckley, James, Jr., 1963- author. | Anderson, Cassie, illustrator.
Title: Fight for life! : rain forest survivor / by James Buckley Jr. ;
   illustrated by Cassie Anderson.
Description: Minneapolis, Minnesota : Bearport Publishing, 2023. | Series:
   The limits of survival | Includes bibliographical references and index.
Identifiers: LCCN 2022002326 (print) | LCCN 2022002327 (ebook) | ISBN
   9781636919898 (library binding) | ISBN 9781636919966 (paperback) | ISBN
   9798885090032 (ebook)
Subjects: LCSH: Koepcke, Juliane--Comic books, strips, etc. | Airplane
   crash survival--Peru--Comic books, strips, etc. | Jungle
   survival--Peru--Comic books, strips, etc. | Graphic novels.
Classification: LCC TL553.9 .B83 2023 (print) | LCC TL553.9 (ebook) | DDC
   363.12/40985--dc23/eng/20220223
LC record available at https://lccn.loc.gov/2022002326
LC ebook record available at https://lccn.loc.gov/2022002327

For more information, write to Bearport Publishing, 5357 Penn Avenue South, Minneapolis, MN 55419. Printed in the United States of America.

CONTENTS

Chapter 1

A Terrible Crash

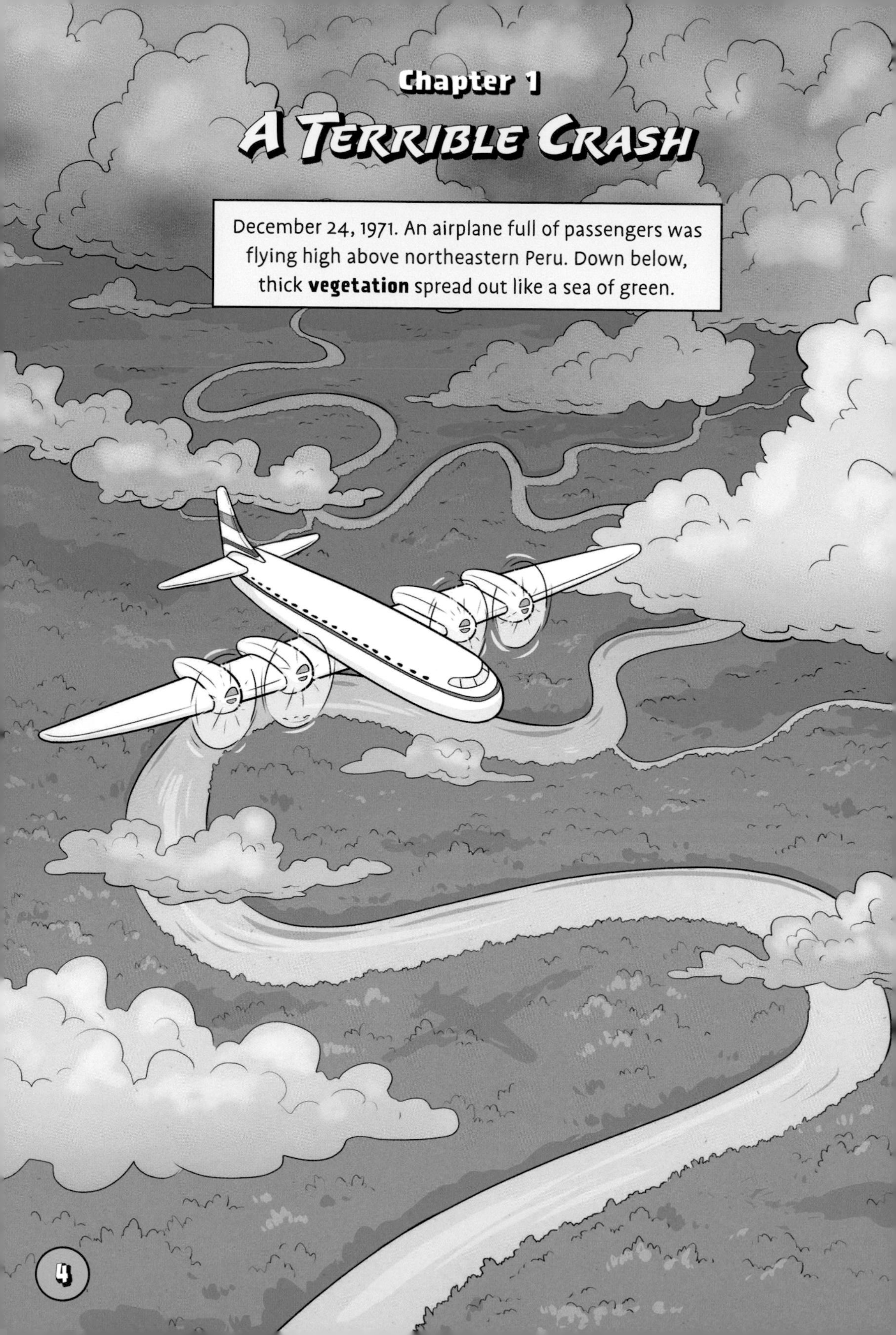
December 24, 1971. An airplane full of passengers was flying high above northeastern Peru. Down below, thick **vegetation** spread out like a sea of green.

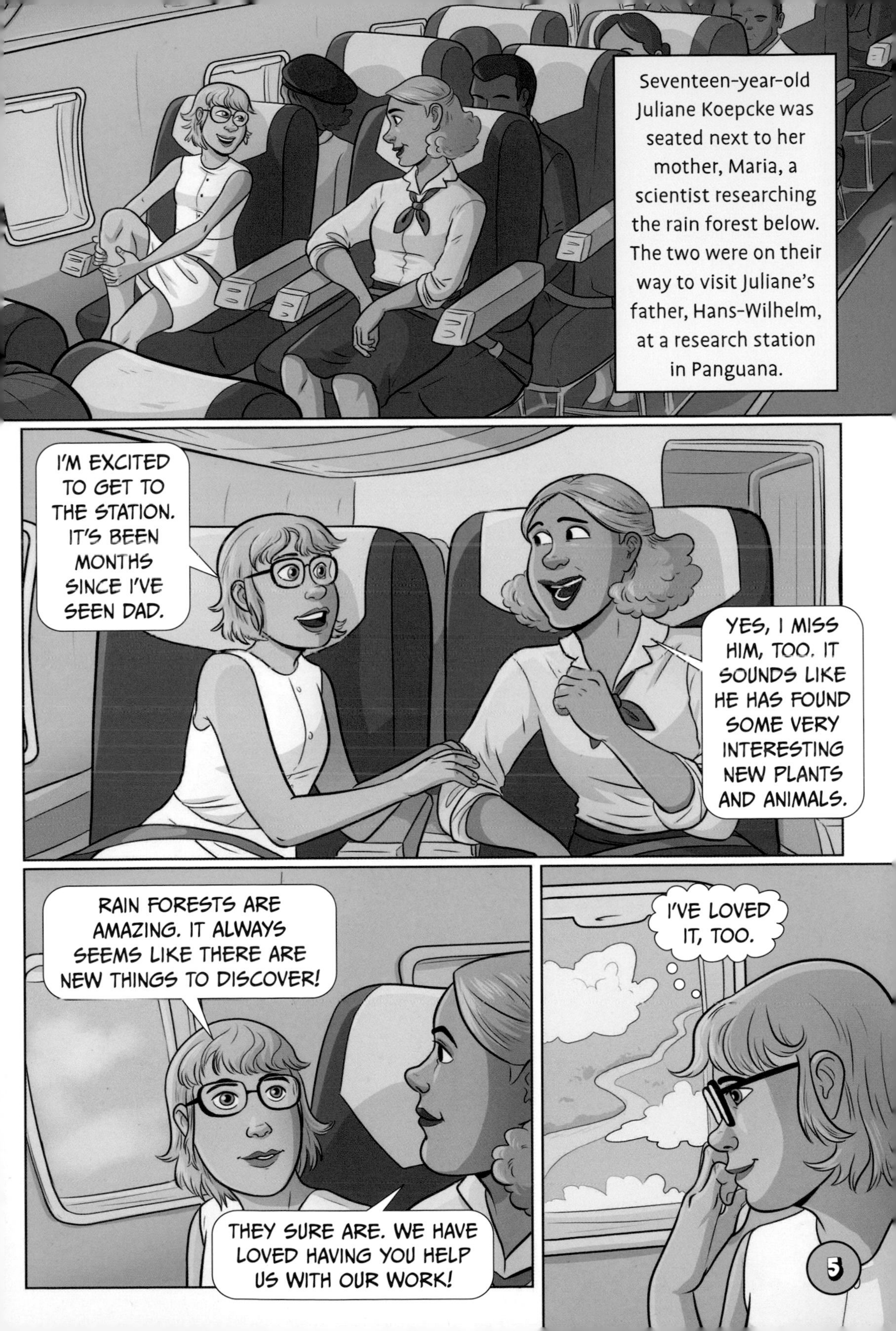
Seventeen-year-old Juliane Koepcke was seated next to her mother, Maria, a scientist researching the rain forest below. The two were on their way to visit Juliane's father, Hans-Wilhelm, at a research station in Panguana.
I'M EXCITED TO GET TO THE STATION. IT'S BEEN MONTHS SINCE I'VE SEEN DAD.
YES, I MISS HIM, TOO. IT SOUNDS LIKE HE HAS FOUND SOME VERY INTERESTING NEW PLANTS AND ANIMALS.
RAIN FORESTS ARE AMAZING. IT ALWAYS SEEMS LIKE THERE ARE NEW THINGS TO DISCOVER!
THEY SURE ARE. WE HAVE LOVED HAVING YOU HELP US WITH OUR WORK!
I'VE LOVED IT, TOO.

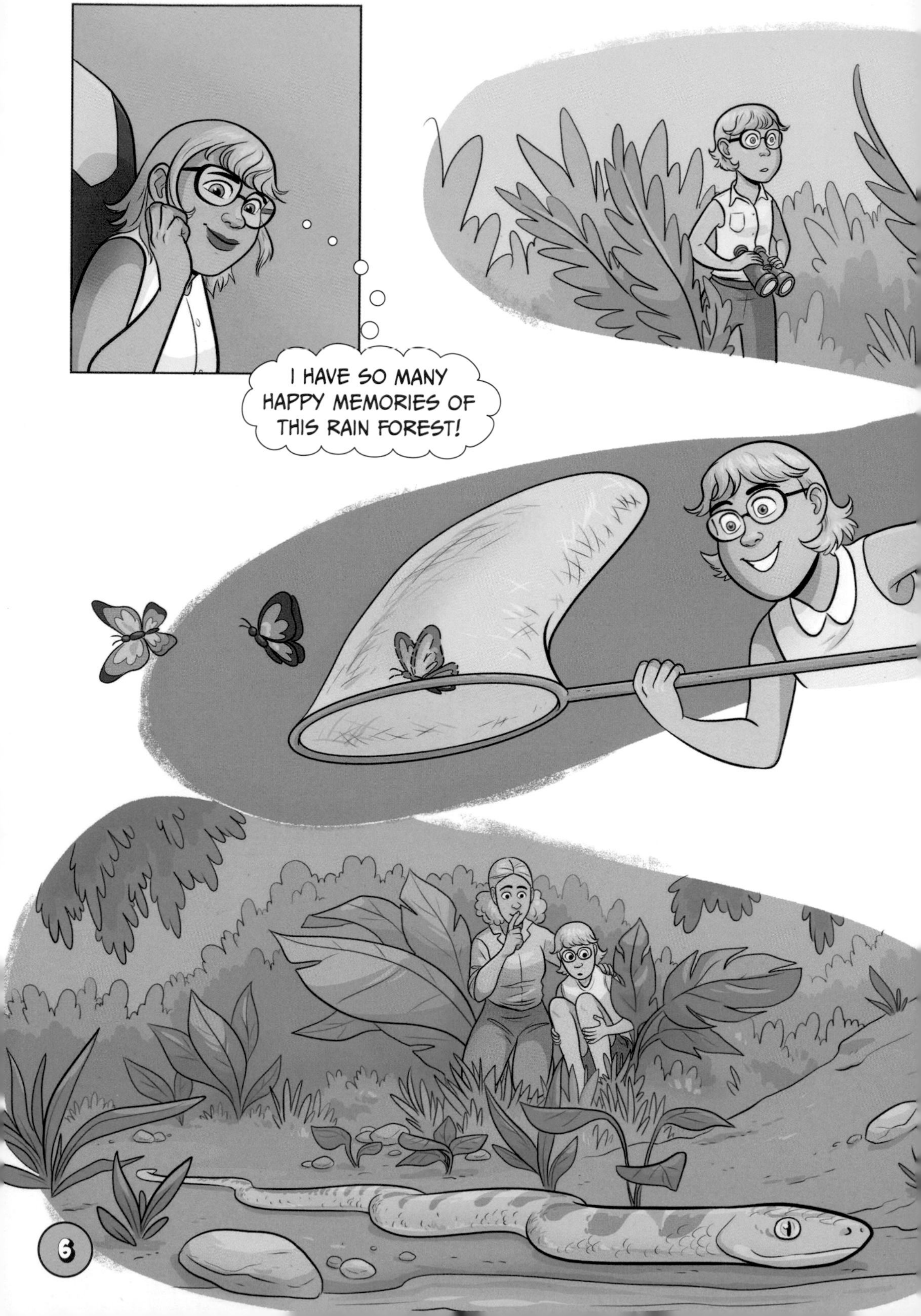
I HAVE SO MANY HAPPY MEMORIES OF THIS RAIN FOREST!

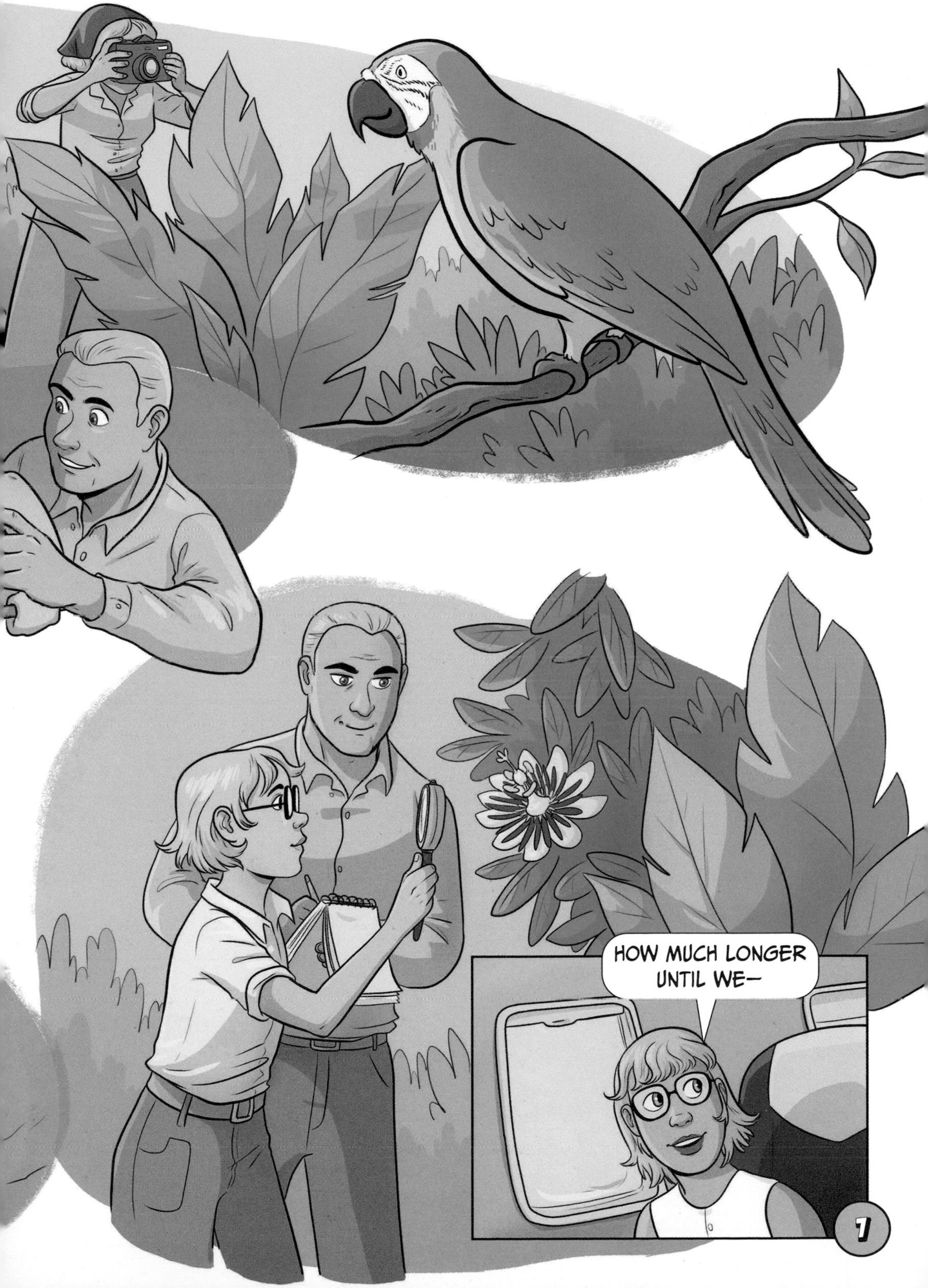
HOW MUCH LONGER UNTIL WE—

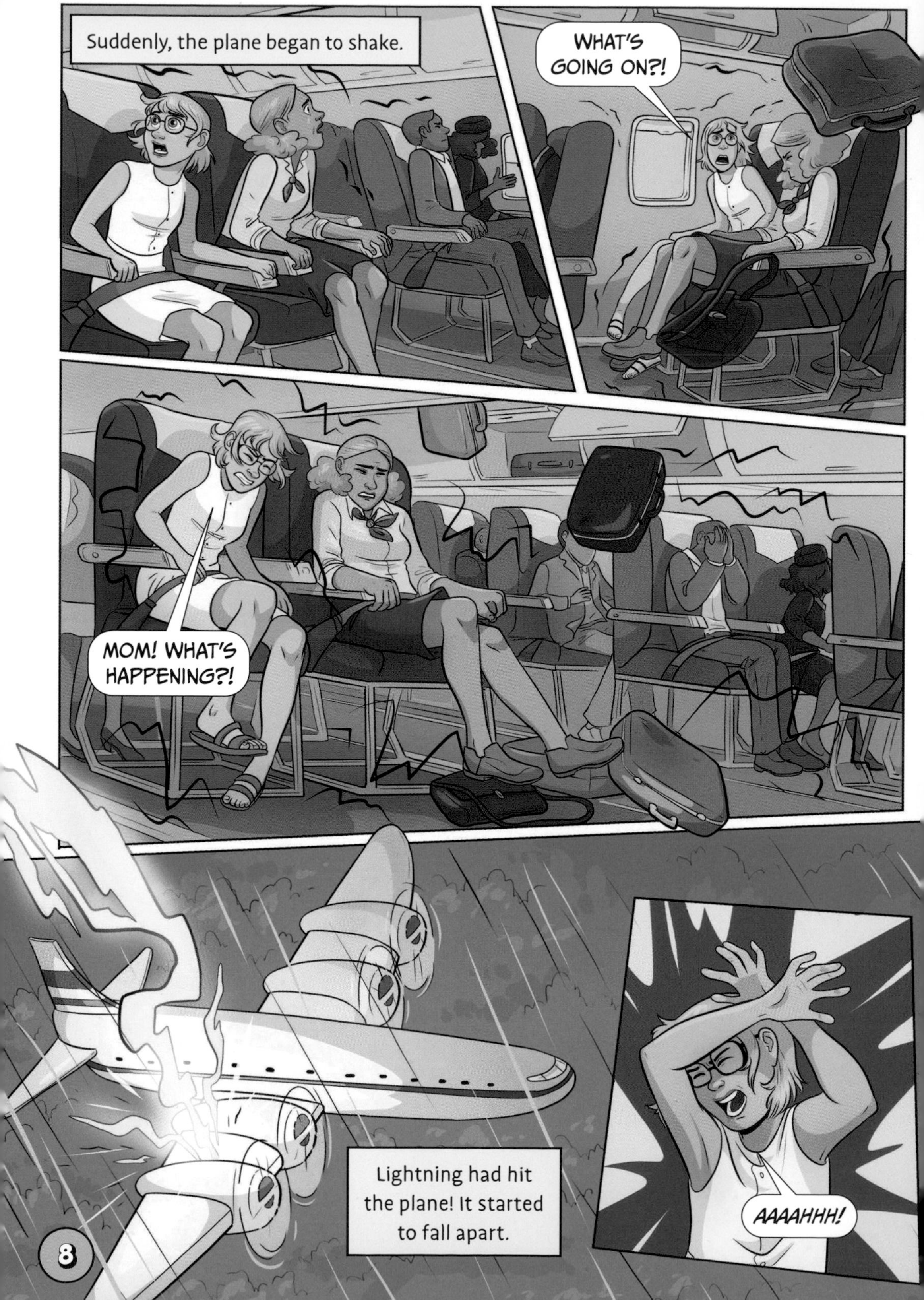

Suddenly, the plane began to shake.
WHAT'S GOING ON?!
MOM! WHAT'S HAPPENING?!
Lightning had hit the plane! It started to fall apart.
AAAAHHH!

The plane fell from the sky almost two miles* down and through the thick **canopy** of the rain forest.

*3 km

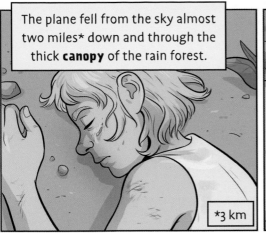

Incredibly, Juliane was alive... but hurt.

Maria and the other passengers were nowhere in sight.

MOM!

MO-OOM! WHERE ARE YOU?!

Juliane knew she was okay for the moment. But she was also very, very alone. She would need to find help.

Chapter 2
The Fight for Survival

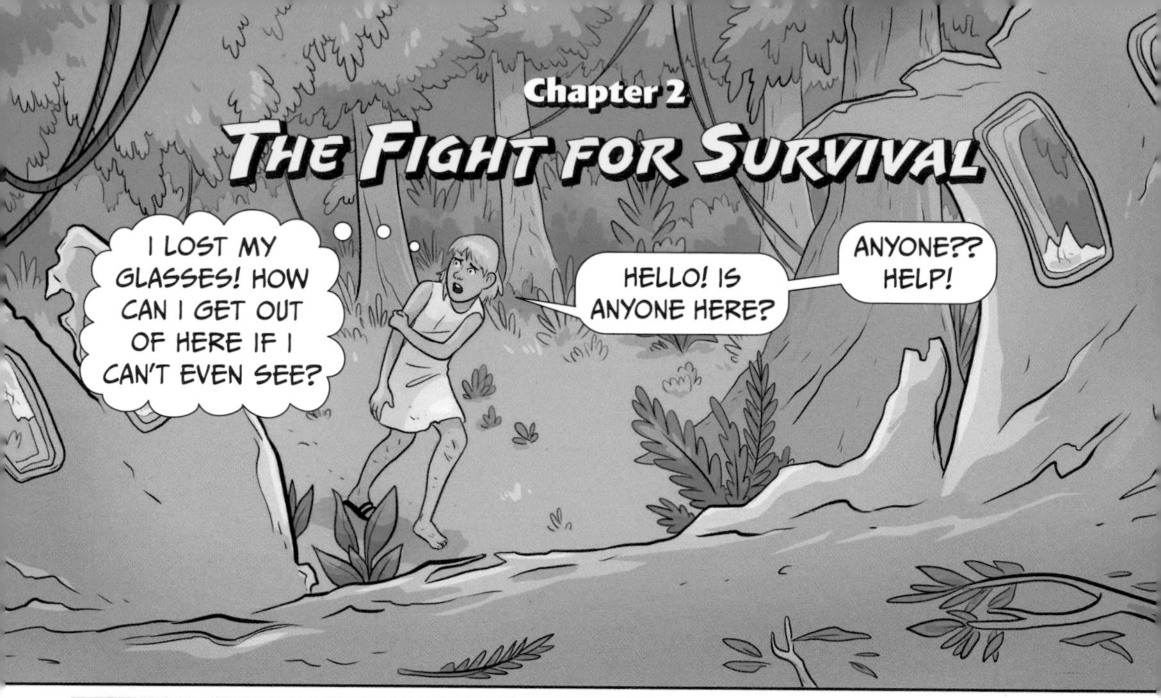

I LOST MY GLASSES! HOW CAN I GET OUT OF HERE IF I CAN'T EVEN SEE?
HELLO! IS ANYONE HERE?
ANYONE?? HELP!

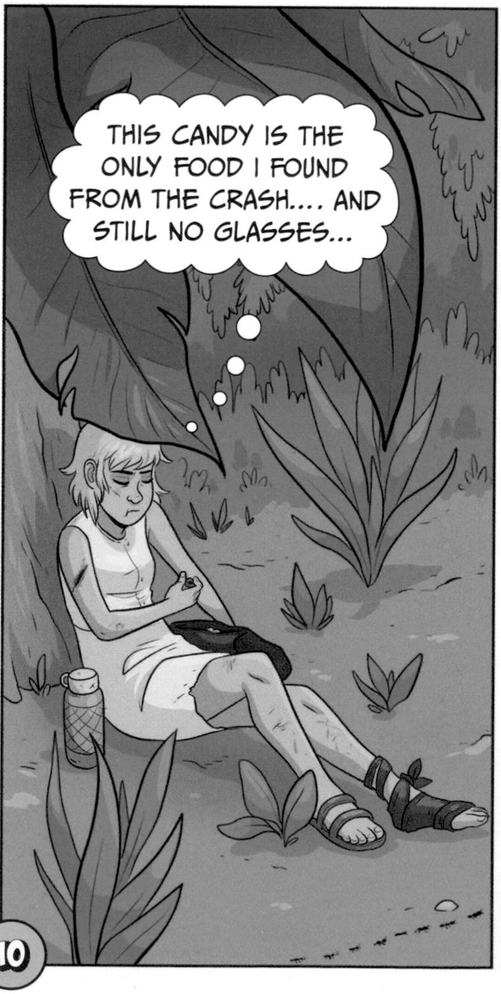

THIS CANDY IS THE ONLY FOOD I FOUND FROM THE CRASH.... AND STILL NO GLASSES...

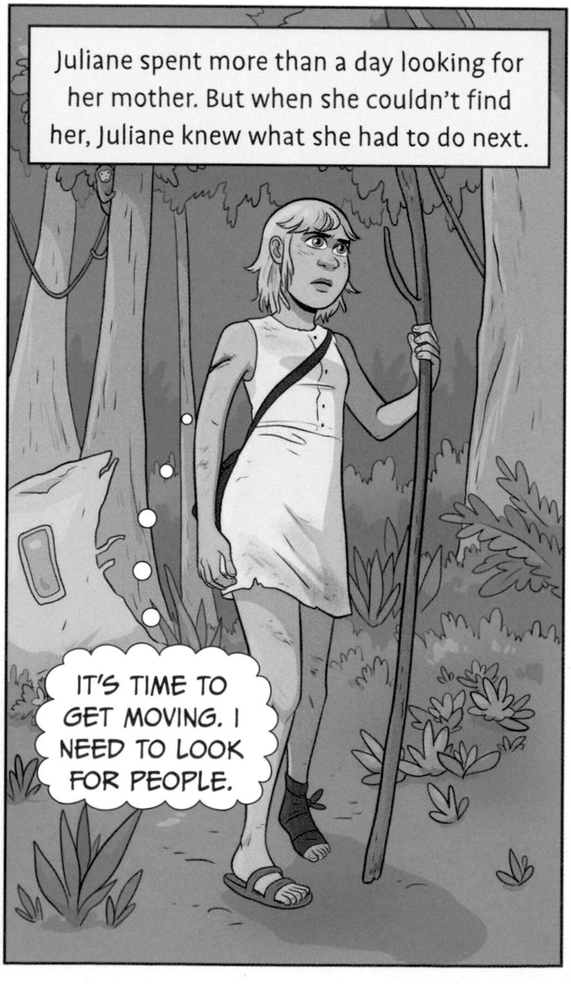

Juliane spent more than a day looking for her mother. But when she couldn't find her, Juliane knew what she had to do next.
IT'S TIME TO GET MOVING. I NEED TO LOOK FOR PEOPLE.

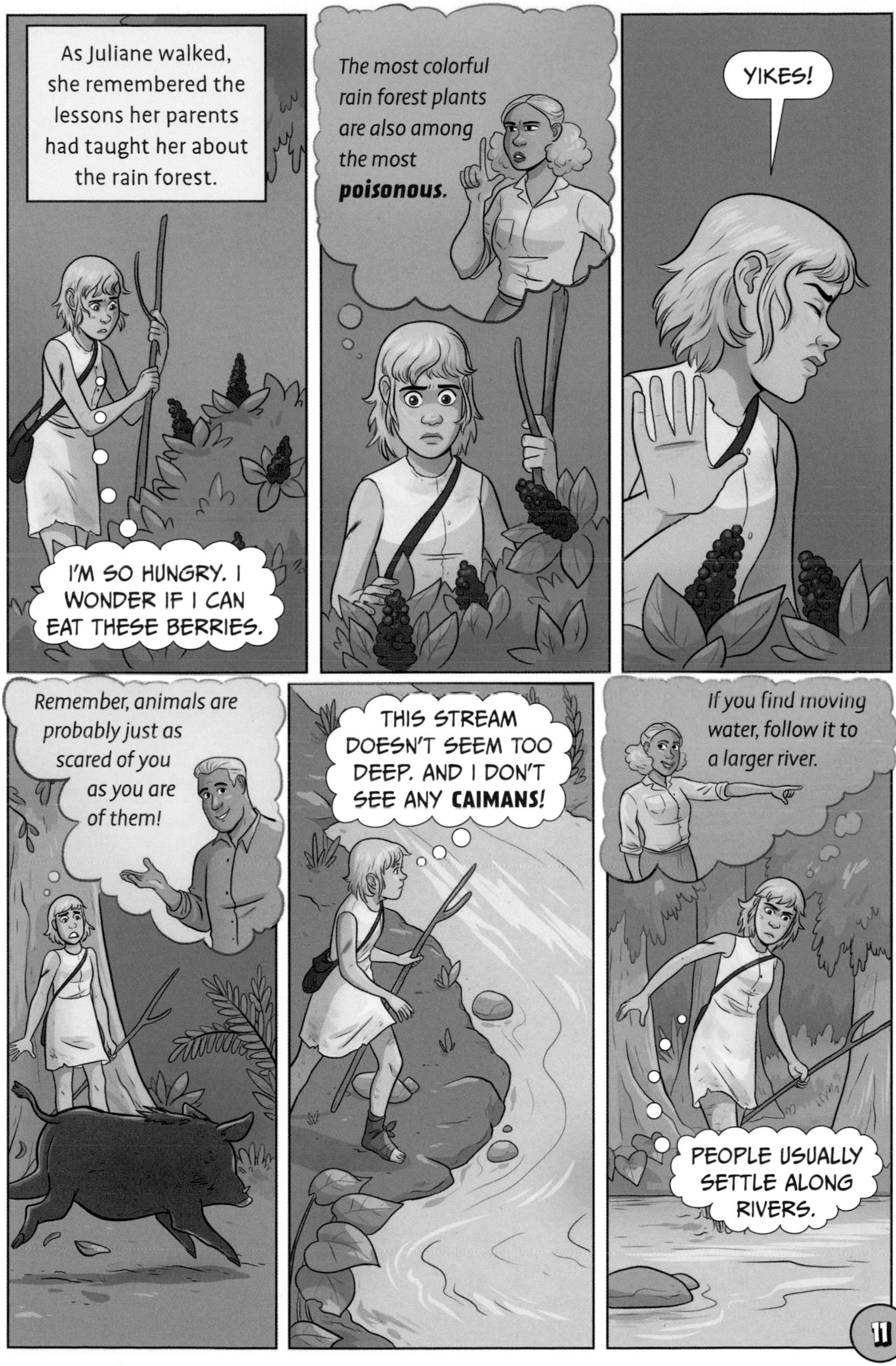
As Juliane walked, she remembered the lessons her parents had taught her about the rain forest.
I'M SO HUNGRY. I WONDER IF I CAN EAT THESE BERRIES.
The most colorful rain forest plants are also among the most **poisonous.**
YIKES!
Remember, animals are probably just as scared of you as you are of them!
THIS STREAM DOESN'T SEEM TOO DEEP. AND I DON'T SEE ANY **CAIMANS!**
If you find moving water, follow it to a larger river.
PEOPLE USUALLY SETTLE ALONG RIVERS.

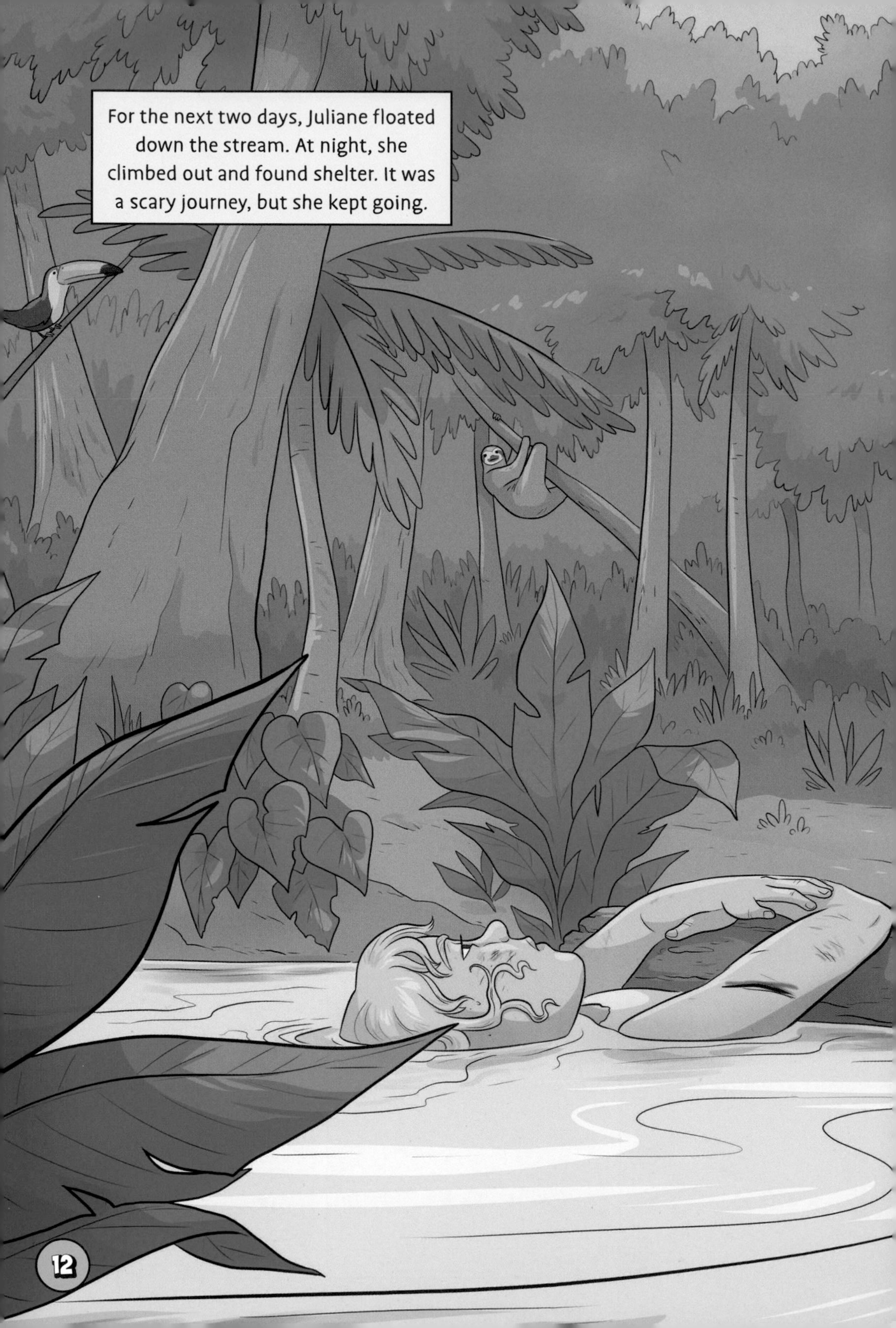
For the next two days, Juliane floated down the stream. At night, she climbed out and found shelter. It was a scary journey, but she kept going.

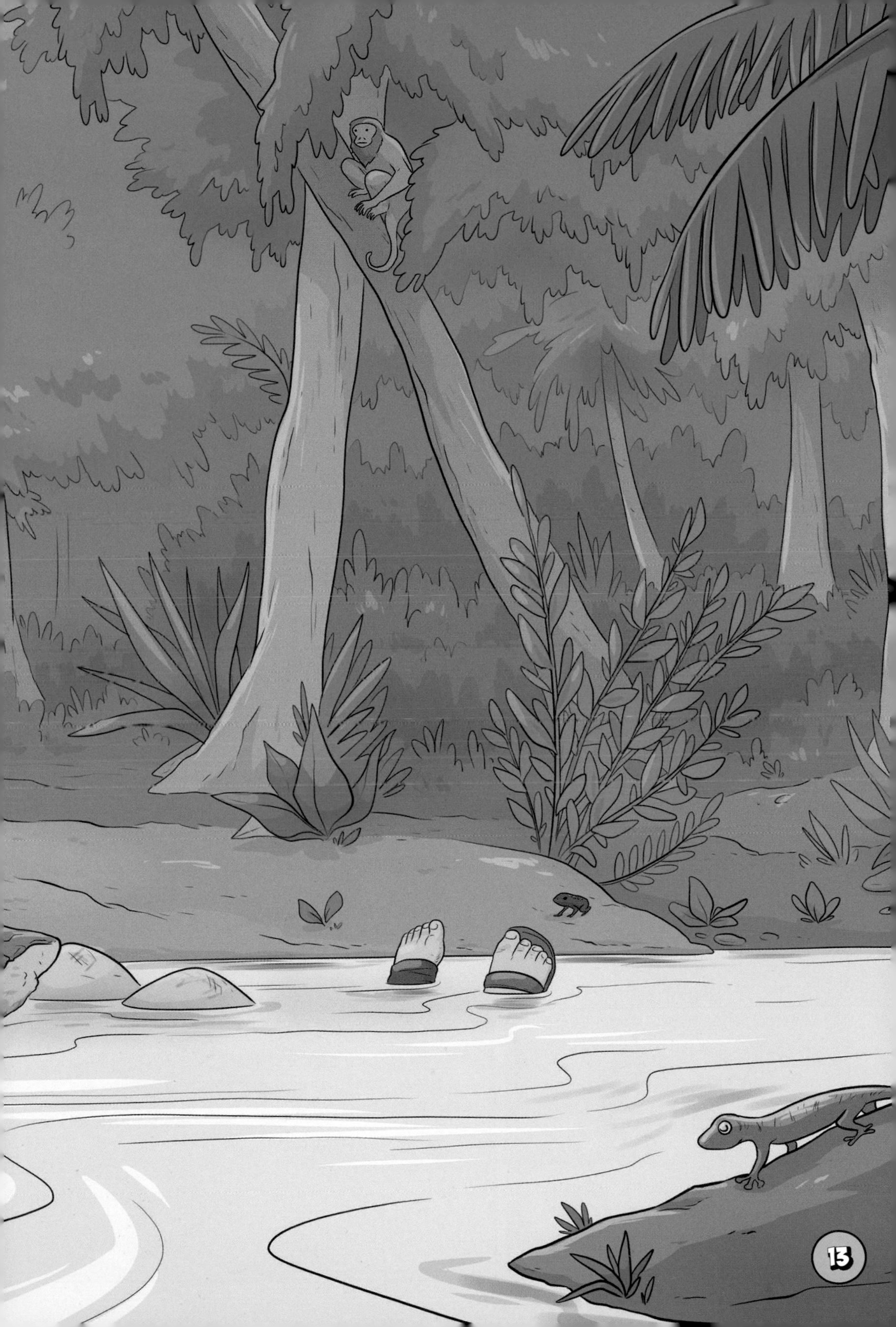

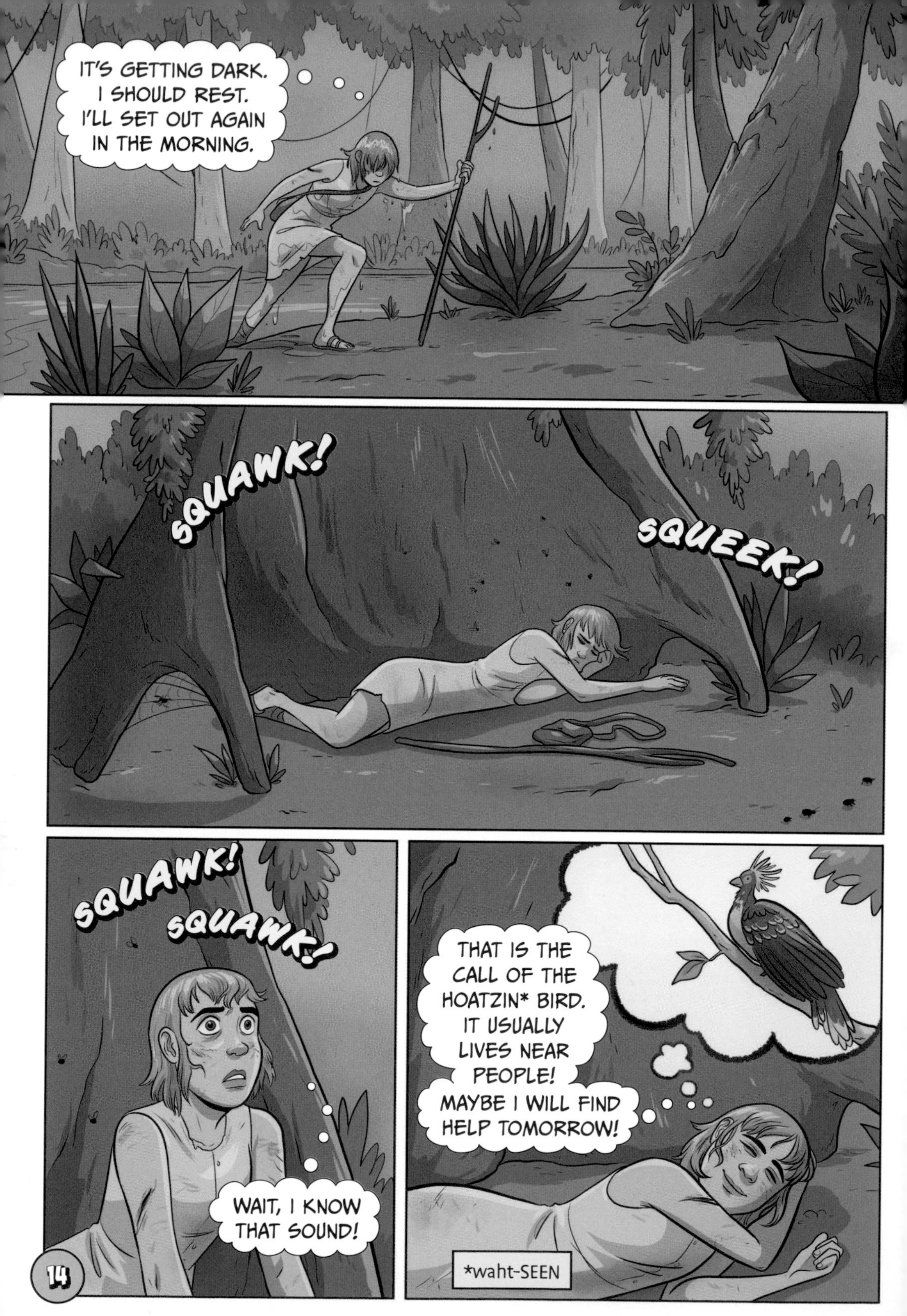
IT'S GETTING DARK. I SHOULD REST. I'LL SET OUT AGAIN IN THE MORNING.
SQUAWK!
SQUEEK!
SQUAWK!
SQUAWK!
WAIT, I KNOW THAT SOUND!
THAT IS THE CALL OF THE HOATZIN* BIRD. IT USUALLY LIVES NEAR PEOPLE! MAYBE I WILL FIND HELP TOMORROW!
*waht-SEEN

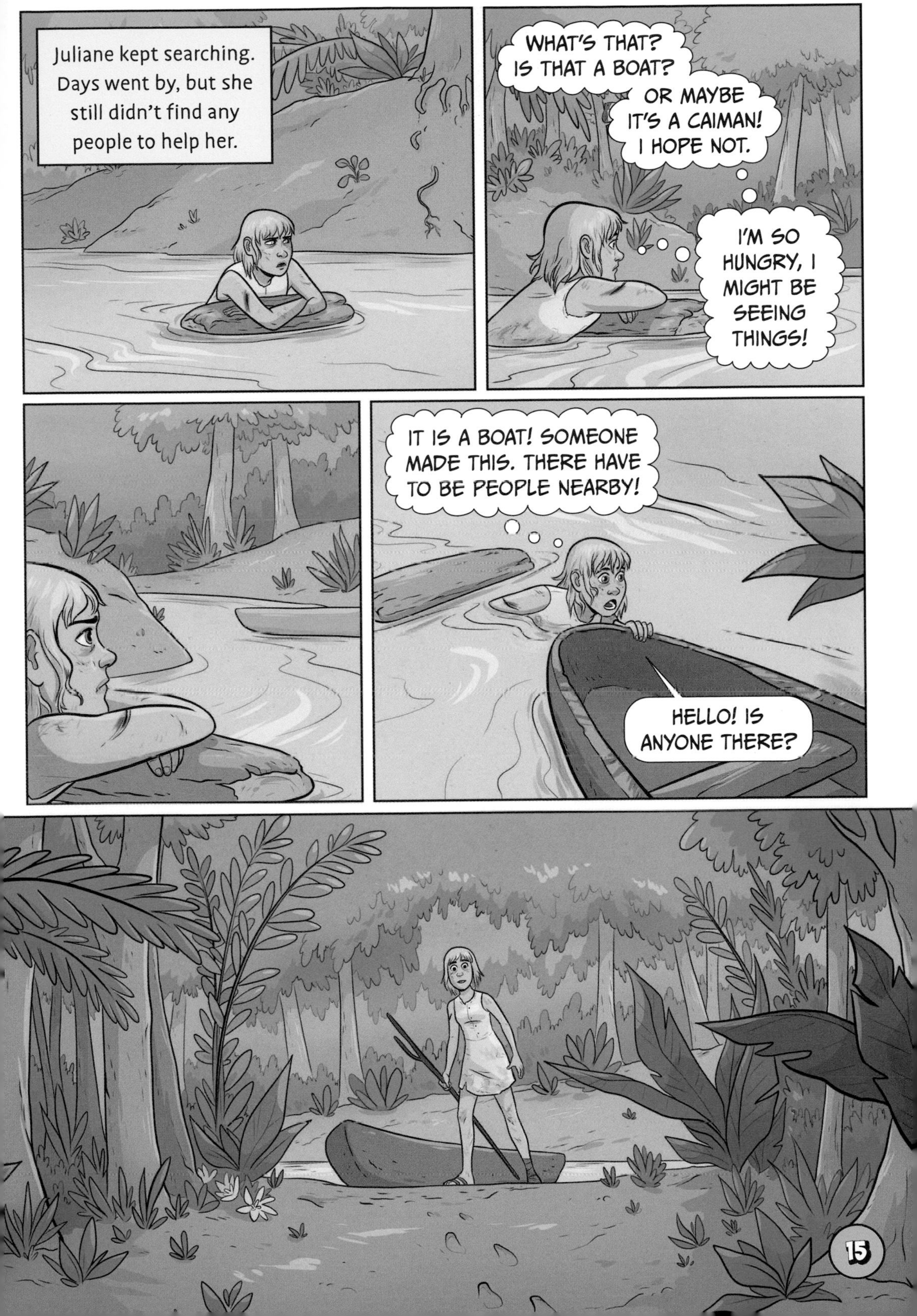

Juliane kept searching. Days went by, but she still didn't find any people to help her.
WHAT'S THAT? IS THAT A BOAT?
OR MAYBE IT'S A CAIMAN! I HOPE NOT.
I'M SO HUNGRY, I MIGHT BE SEEING THINGS!
IT IS A BOAT! SOMEONE MADE THIS. THERE HAVE TO BE PEOPLE NEARBY!
HELLO! IS ANYONE THERE?

Chapter 3
Safe at Last

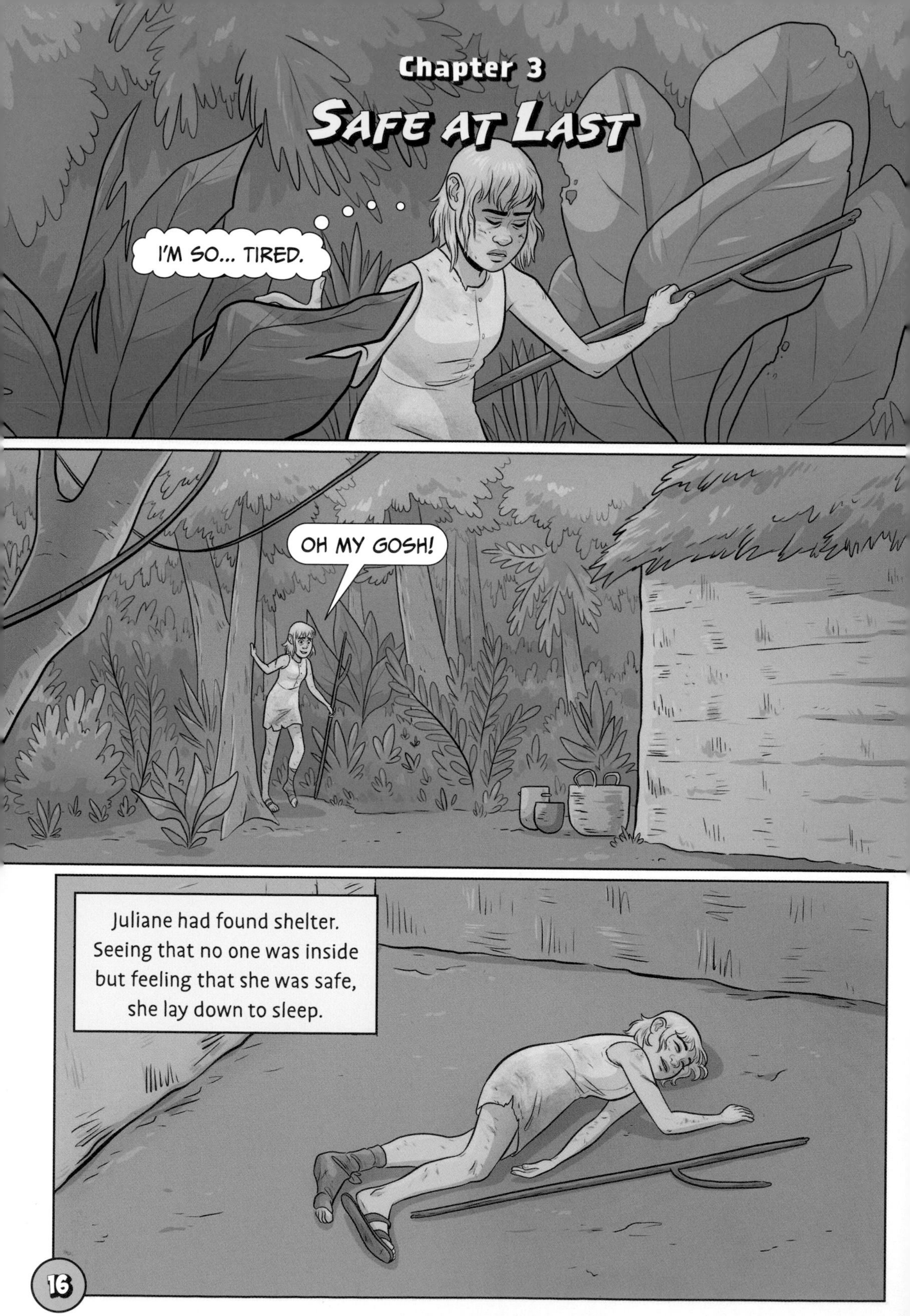
I'M SO... TIRED.
OH MY GOSH!
Juliane had found shelter. Seeing that no one was inside but feeling that she was safe, she lay down to sleep.

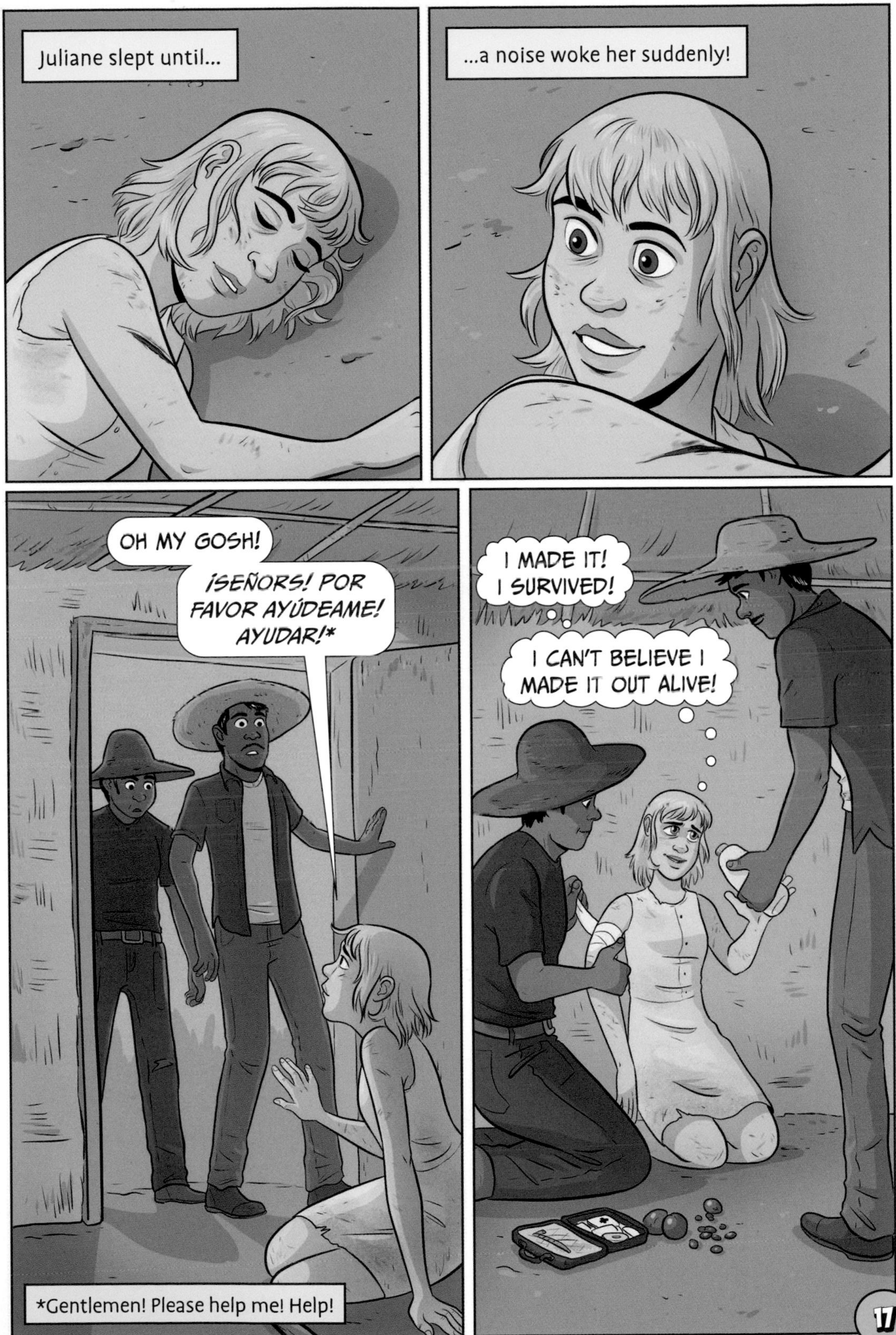
Juliane slept until...
...a noise woke her suddenly!
OH MY GOSH!
¡SEÑORS! POR FAVOR AYÚDEAME! AYUDAR!*
*Gentlemen! Please help me! Help!
I MADE IT! I SURVIVED!
I CAN'T BELIEVE I MADE IT OUT ALIVE!

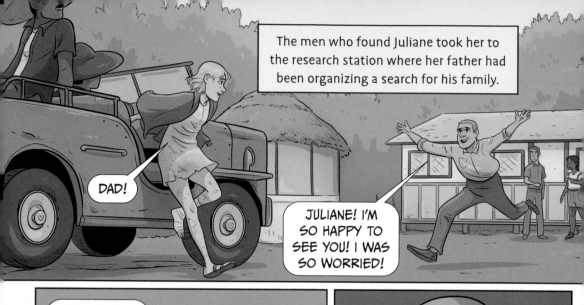

The men who found Juliane took her to the research station where her father had been organizing a search for his family.

DAD!

JULIANE! I'M SO HAPPY TO SEE YOU! I WAS SO WORRIED!

HAS MOM BEEN FOUND?

YES, BUT I'M AFRAID IT'S BAD NEWS. SHE WAS KILLED IN THE CRASH.

THANK GOODNESS YOU COULD HELP HER. SHE HAS BEEN OUT THERE FOR 11 DAYS!

INCREDIBLE! SHE IS A BRAVE YOUNG WOMAN, SIR.

Juliane was the only person to survive the plane crash.

She also survived the rain forest.

18

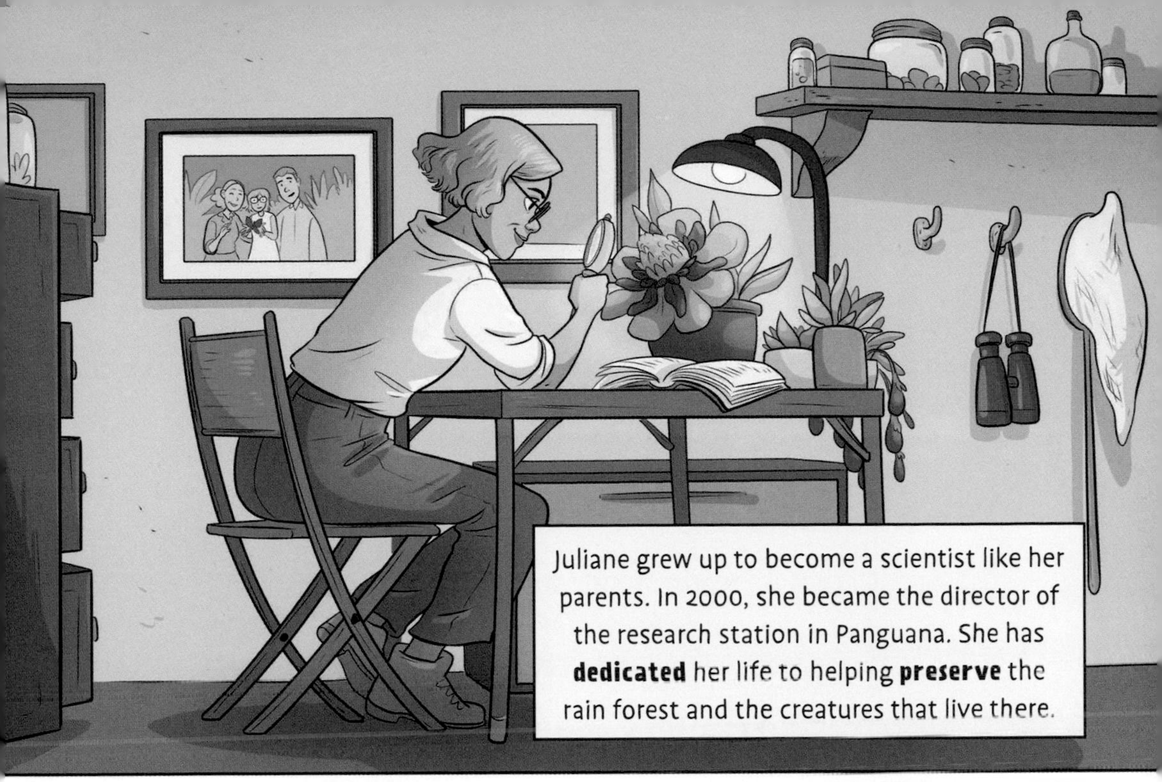
Juliane grew up to become a scientist like her parents. In 2000, she became the director of the research station in Panguana. She has **dedicated** her life to helping **preserve** the rain forest and the creatures that live there.

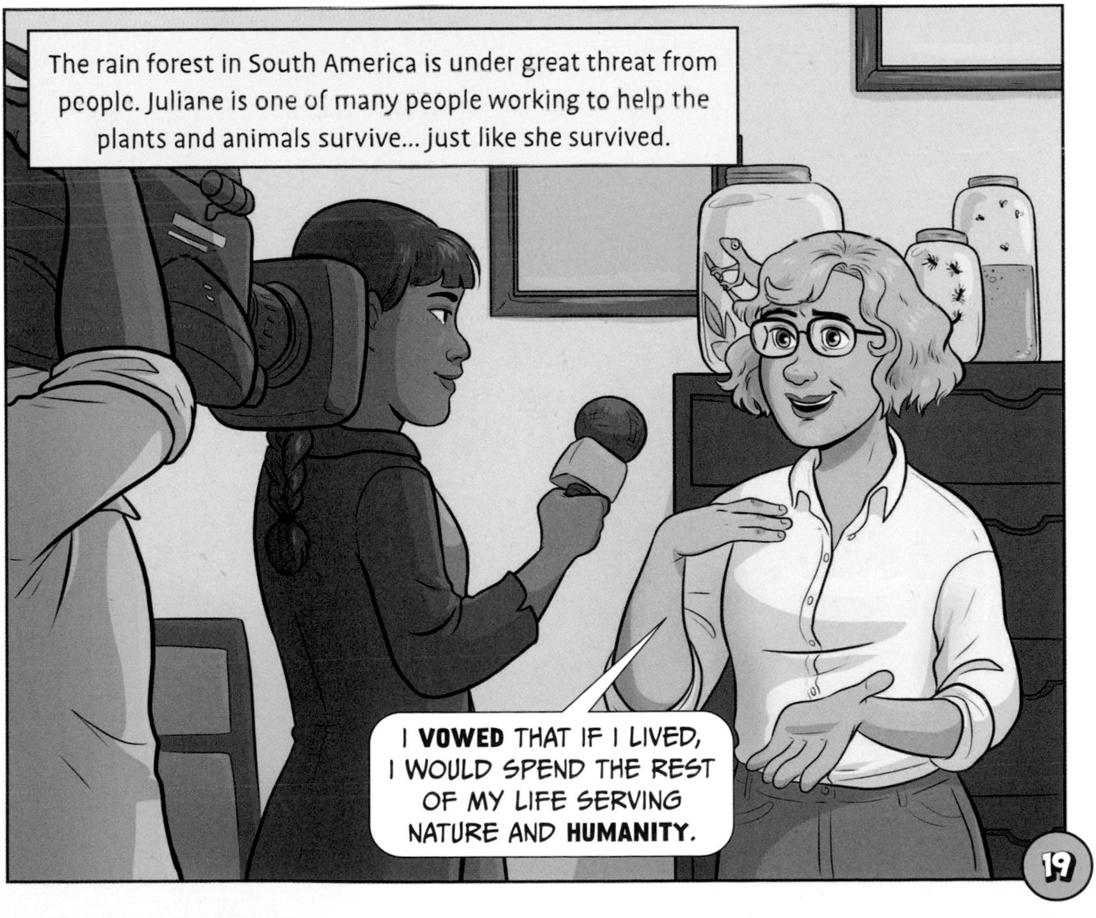
The rain forest in South America is under great threat from people. Juliane is one of many people working to help the plants and animals survive... just like she survived.
I **VOWED** THAT IF I LIVED, I WOULD SPEND THE REST OF MY LIFE SERVING NATURE AND **HUMANITY**.

Rain Forest Survival Tips

If you plan to visit a rain forest, follow these tips to help you survive.

- Tell people where you are going and when you expect to be back so they'll know where to look if you get lost.
- Wear clothes for warm, humid weather. You may have to walk in puddles, so wear waterproof shoes or wrap your shoes in plastic bags. Keep your skin covered to avoid scratches and insect bites.

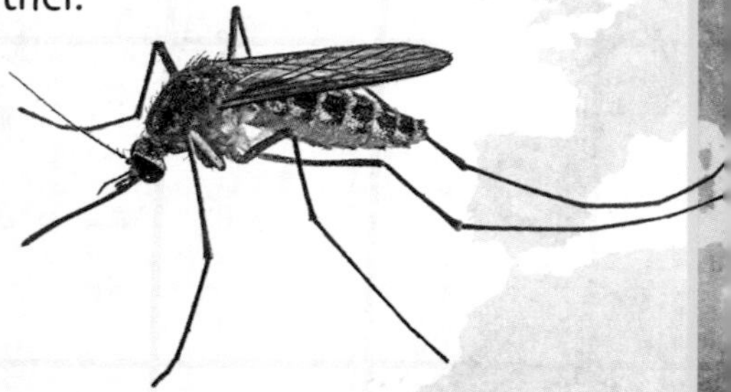

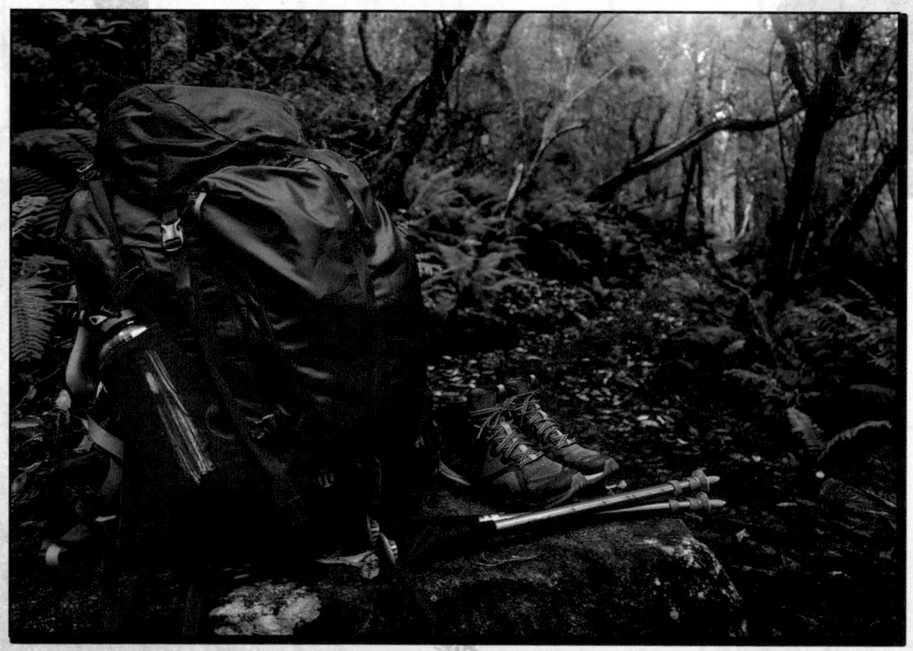

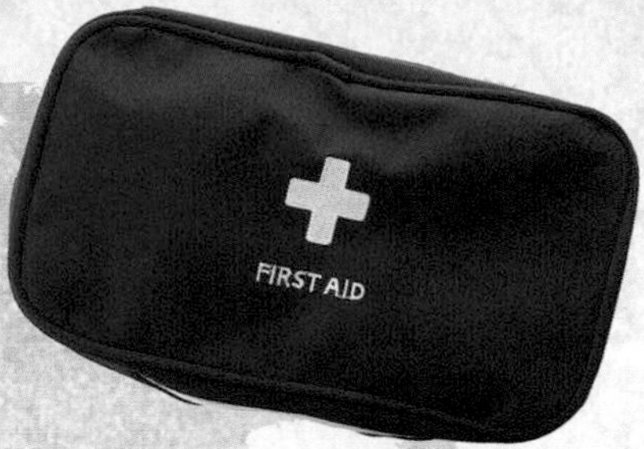
FIRST AID

- Pack a first-aid kit, a compass, a map, a knife, and a flashlight. Bring bottled water and canned or dried food.
- Bring matches, lighters, or a flint to start a fire in order to cook food, stay warm, scare off predators, and alert people that you are stranded.
- Before hiking, look for a long stick. Use it to push aside leaves and branches. It can also help you keep your balance on uneven ground.
- If you're on a hill, move downhill to look for fresh water. Drink only from fast-flowing streams.
- If you need to look for food in the rain forest, eat only things you know are safe, such as coconuts or citrus fruits.

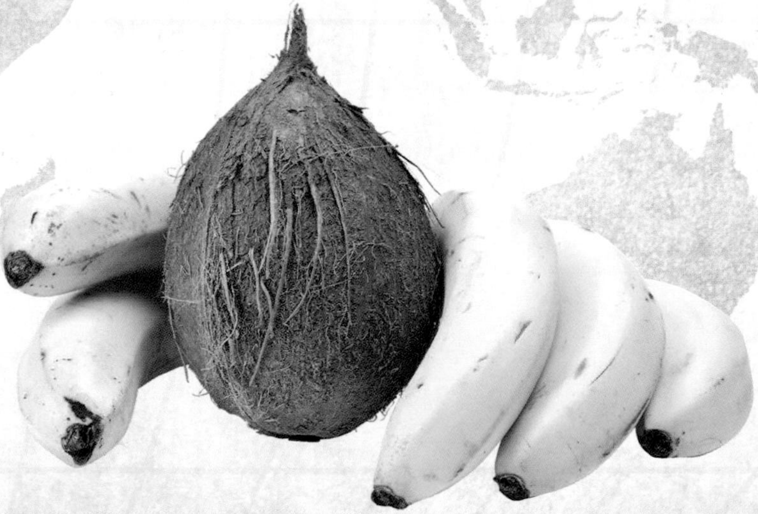

OTHER RAIN FOREST SURVIVORS

Brandon and Brandy Wiley also survived after their plane crashed in a rain forest. They climbed out of the plane and found other survivors. Brandy was a nurse, so she was able to help the injured. Together, the group gathered what they could

from the crash. At night, they started a fire to attract attention. Finally, a rescuer **hacked** through the jungle to help bring the couple and the other survivors to safety.

For Shannon Fraser, a day at a watering hole in the Australian rain forest turned into almost three weeks of fear. She got lost after stepping away from her friends during their day out. For the next 17 days, she wandered while people searched for her. She survived by drinking river water and eating fish, as well as insects. Eventually, she found her way back to safety.

GLOSSARY

caimans South American reptiles that are related to alligators

canopy the layer of rain forest growth that is farthest from the ground

dedicated devoted to something important

hacked chopped with a sharp blade

humanity all human beings together

poisonous dangerous or deadly when eaten

preserve to keep around for the future

vegetation plant life

vowed made a solemn promise

Index

Read More

Hudak, Heather. *Rainforest Survival Guide (Brave the Biome).* New York: Crabtree Publishing, 2021.

Huddleston, Emma. *Looking into the Rain Forest (Looking at Layers).* Mankato, MN: The Child's World, 2020.

Klepeis, Alicia Z. *Living in the Rain Forest (How Do You Live There?!).* New York: PowerKids Press, 2021.

Learn More Online

1. Go to **www.factsurfer.com** or scan the QR code below.

2. Enter **"Fight for Life"** into the search box.

3. Click on the cover of this book to see a list of websites.